AWAKE SOULS

A COLLECTION OF POEMS

SUHAYL

MAPLE
PUBLISHERS

Awakening Souls – A Collection of Poems

Author: Suhayl

Copyright © 2024 Suhayl

The right of Suhayl to be identified as author of this work has been asserted by the author in accordance with section 77 and 78 of the Copyright, Designs and Patents Act 1988.

ISBN 978-1-83538-363-6 (Paperback)
      978-1-83538-364-3 (E-Book)

Cover Design and Book Layout by:
    White Magic Studios
    www.whitemagicstudios.co.uk

Published by:
    Maple Publishers
    Fairbourne Drive, Atterbury,
    Milton Keynes,
    MK10 9RG, UK
    www.maplepublishers.com

Acknowledgement

I want to express my gratitude to everyone who has supported and guided me—teachers, poets, colleagues, friends, and family.

Thanks to Maple publishers for helping me publish my first collection.

A special thanks to my parents for raising me with love and discipline, shaping the man I am today.

I'm ever grateful to my wife for her unwavering belief, patience, and encouragement; this journey is as much yours as it is mine.

To my children, thank you for bringing joy and sunshine into my life.

Most importantly, I thank Allah for His countless blessings upon me.

Contents

INTRODUCTION

Throughout life, many face challenges with quiet resilience and unwavering courage, often away from the public eye. Their stories are rarely told, their struggles seldom acknowledged, yet their strength leaves a profound impact on the world around them. It is this quiet perseverance that inspired these words.

As these pages unfold, the hope is to bring such stories to light— to recognize the courage that often goes unseen and to encourage a deeper understanding of the battles many face in silence. This work aims to foster greater empathy, compassion, and awareness for those whose journeys are frequently overlooked.

For those who carry on despite the weight of their struggles, who find light in the darkest moments, and who rise each day with renewed strength, may these words serve as a recognition of the resilience that shapes the world in ways both small and great. The goal is for these experiences to be seen, heard, and appreciated, as they so rightfully deserve.

Suhayl

INTRODUCTION

HOUSE OF MERCY

HOUSE OF MERCY

Come, you who are afraid,
And seek shelter from the rain.
Come, if your heart is weary,
To find solace in your pain.
Come, you with broken spirit,
Allow yourself to mend.
Come, the rejected and alone,
Here, you shan't be condemned.
Come, even if you cannot come,
Let your soul be your guide,
Come.

FAITHLESS ALLIANCE

FAITHLESS ALLIANCE

I want to pay tribute to the governments,
And their loyal and faithful allies, the media.
Thank you from the very bottom of my heart,
For being such staunch promoters of inequality.
Thank you for your dishonesty and insincerity.
Thank you for taking a stand against justice,
And relentlessly pursuing injustice.
Thank you for speaking up for the powerful,
And making voiceless the weak.
Thank you for condemning the victims,
And aiding their oppressors every step of the way,
Reminding us of their right to defend.
Last but not least,
Thank you for bringing pain and misery to the world.
Thank you, thank you, thank you!

THE DEVIL'S HEAVEN

THE DEVIL'S HEAVEN

It was never meant to be like this,
A marriage made from happiness,
Loving everything you offered me,
Believing this my destiny,
Obeying all your rituals,
Feelings, said were mutual,
Following all your crazy trends,
Promoted by your crazy friends,
Who themselves, are deceived,
What they see, they don't perceive,
I couldn't bear the pain no more,
I've seen you play these games before,
I couldn't compromise no more,
The light too bright to let it go,
It wasn't easy, you held me tight,
But freedom was mine, it was my right.

So release me from these chains,
Let me purify my tainted soul.
The devil's heaven is not for me,
Rather die free, than live till old

THE DEVIL'S HEAVEN

You can't convince me otherwise,
The flames been lit, no cowards eyes,
Your charm won't work, O wicked flirt,
I'm now so clean, don't need your dirt,
You have so many unknowing slaves,
Some living blind, some to be saved,
All victims of your system,
Helpless to your addiction,
Born into this world of sin,
Forced to fight demons within,
But many have chosen life,
We'll have to make the sacrifice.

So release me from these chains,
Let me purify my tainted soul.
The devil's heaven is not for me,
Rather die free, than live till old.

Story behind the poem

The poem **Signs in the Design** (on p. 20) poses a heartfelt question to those who doubt the presence of a higher power. It points to the remarkable complexity of the universe, suggesting that such complexity could not have come into being by mere chance.

SOUL

SOUL

A billion souls grow,
But only some
truly blossom.

MY LOVE

MY LOVE

I will touch the depths of the deep,
And scale the most mightiest peaks.
I will inhale the worst toxic fumes,
And wait patiently in the loneliest gloom.
All this to be with you my love.

There is no-one else, but you I desire.
You are the spark that ignites my fire.
My heart pounds my chest when we're alone.
Such pride is felt to call you my own.
I'd do anything to keep you my love.

You'd do anything for me, this I know.
Promise to hold me tight, and never let go.
Your presence calms even my weakest nerves.
My everything is yours, still more you deserve.
I want nothing more than you my love.

SIGNS IN THE DESIGN

There are too many signs,
To prove the divine.
One of the greatest of these,
Is the intelligent design.
Take a long look,
Or simply a glance.
Did this perfection,
Truly come by chance?

COME WIND, BRING ME JOY

Lately, the air has been silent,
The atmosphere that I abhor.
The absence compounded by Men,
Who ever only desire more.

No word can define this pain,
Never a moment passes when,
I reminisce of the era of gain,
And ponder why it left me then.

The day's filled with plenty-less,
Wind, blow away my sorrow.
Come, throw down this emptiness.
I cannot wait till tomorrow.

Lead me from this lifeless doubt,
And away from this perilous ploy.
I am nigh-on finished without,
Come wind, and bring me joy.

DEATH SHALL TAKE YOU

DEATH SHALL TAKE YOU

Death shall take you without warning,
Away from all you hold dear.
Beware of departing unloved,
Leaving many unspoken words.

Ever smile,
For it may be your last.
Carry mercy within your heart,
Hold forgiveness upon your lips,
Wash away your evil deeds,
Replace them with love, and prayers.
Speak ill of no soul,
It merely burdens your grave,
For death will take you,
Leaving you with much regret.

Death shall certainly come,
Snatch you away from redemption,
Allowing no time to make amends.
Beware of death my friend

TODAY I HAVE LEARNED

TODAY I HAVE LEARNED

Love truly happens,

Today I have learned.

Tears can become oceans,

Today I have learned.

Unknowing was I to the insomnia called love,

But love truly happens,

Today I have learned.

MUHAMMAD (PBUH)

MUHAMMAD (PBUH)

His Fathers eyes he never saw,
His Mother taken while so young,
A fragile orphan in that world of Men,
Such patience on that blessed tongue.

He was the pious unlettered one,
For whom was made the moon and sun,
He was the most greatest Man,
For whom the Lord had made a plan.

His demeanor, neither rash nor cruel,
Rather, was most calm and kind.
Search through the first until the last,
An equal you shall never find.

PAUPER AND KING

The prayer of
A Pauper
Is more precious
Than gold from
A King.

I SHALL RISE

I SHALL RISE

Disgrace me, nay destroy,
Yet as one with many lives,
From the depths of evil ploys,
Unto lofty peaks I'll rise.

Every sane would crave release,
From the hell that has become,
Yet I reject these mortal wounds,
And vow to ever rise.
Recalling tales of fearless struggle,
Whose spirits oceans vast,
Indeed my desire to become alike,
And be raised
Amid the givers of sacrifice,
Who rejoice over my fate
And know,
I surely did rise.

Granted, warm stars do fall,
At dusk's silent cries,
Yet upon dawns serene call,
As the sun I too shall rise.

GREATNESS HIS ALONE

GREATNESS HIS ALONE

Bountiful master of the earth,
Infinite wisdom atop the throne,
Moulded existence from lifeless dirt,
Eternal greatness be his alone.

Be in awe of natures wonder,
Radiant vastness of oceans deep,
Skies of rain, likewise thunder,
Endless plains and mighty peaks.

Ponder on the many signs,
Blessings from the ever grand,
Search in earnest you shall find,
Beyond the seen a noble hand.

WE SHALL

WE SHALL

A mighty foe lay siege upon us.
Indeed a far greater peril
Than those resisted.
Unrelenting in his quest,
Unwavering in his hatred,
Unyielding in his resolve,
Unabashed in his deception,
Striking at each and every turn,
His enticement seldom refused,
Enduring endless millennia,
To sow seeds of division.

Only the unwise pay no heed to our destruction,
Lest we fall.
To our fate lest we are conquered.
If we dare fail, then I tremble,
Oh I tremble with the known and unknown,
With the unseen and foreseen,
I tremble with the whispers of defeat,
"Ye shall be deceived, divided, devoured."

WE SHALL

Shall this our destiny become?

No!

Far content with the scent of death than disgrace.

We shall abolish all fear within,

We shall implore the supreme,

We shall persist along this road fraught with devastation,

We shall march forth with steadfast purpose,

We shall remain unified,

We shall triumph albeit weary,

With firm faith and iron will,

We shall amass!

We shall arise!

We shall attain!

This our destiny shall become!

Story behind the poem

A poem that honours women everywhere, celebrating their strength and dignity. It emphasizes that a woman's royalty comes not from her lineage, but from her virtues and deeds. By embracing her true self, she can realize her full potential and discover her **Inner Crown** (on p. 80)

KING AND QUEEN

KING AND QUEEN

A heavenly and fragile dove,
Shields herself within his love.
A bond grander than any seen,
A noble king, a pious queen,
Content within a perfect dream,
A blessed union from above.

FOREVER MY MOTHER

A Man of firmest spirit I am,
Mighty alike the trees I stand,
Virility smiles boldly upon me,
In my presence fear takes leave,
My every stride is one of valour,
Yet still I possess her tenderness.
Her essence surrounds me.
Her gentle soul flows within me.
Her blessing is my tranquility.
Every comfort lies at her feet,
Every treasure is lost before her beauty.
She is the sanity in my madness,
She is the calm in my rage
She is the lamp alighting my darkness,
She is my every pureness,
Forever, my Mother.

HONOUR AND BLOOD

HONOUR AND BLOOD

When ours was might,
And none was theirs.
We clothed weakness,
And nourished frailty.
We sheltered them from every foe,
Who sought to shackle their tongue.
Each Hebrew verse was liberated,
And guarded faithfully,
As Kin guard Kin,
With honour and blood.

Now might be theirs,
And none be ours.
All hope is entombed,
And liberty enchained.
Each right tortured,
And promise betrayed.
Severed be the Fatherland,
Within solitude it decays,
Truth but a mere known,
Justice but a mere name.

Though our nation lay divided,
Our spirits are eternally bound.
We shall arise and overcome.
We shall endure and oppose,
As valiantly as we once guarded,
With honour and blood.

Story behind the poem

The theme of the poem **Fire** (on p. 84) reflects how the same force can have dual purposes—both good and evil. Using fire as a metaphor, it shows how it can offer warmth and safety, or cause harm and devastation, depending on how it's wielded.

AN ANGEL CAME

AN ANGEL CAME

Today I woke within my dream,
An angel stood not far from me,
He spoke with ever merry tone,
To tell me that a light had shone,
One further joy along with thee,
Now you shall never be alone.

CONQUERED PRIDE

CONQUERED PRIDE

With faithful toil ye be sav'd,
By tyrants unto fearful slaves.
Weary eyed in shackles deep,
Dreary labours dawn till sleep.
O distant nay indeed decay'd,
Each memory with passing day,
Of joyful kin and freedom good,
Of fervent land once honor stood.
Now every breath in lasting pain,
Eternal ache for ceaseless gain.

Do not despair O conquered pride,
Truth shall evoke each shameless lie.
O unbound soul enchain'd in life,
Time shall unveil each sacrifice.

VIRTUOUS AIM

VIRTUOUS AIM

A belief if be sincere indeed,
Upon oneself be centered not,
For good to rise within each sin,
And light to shine beyond each dark,
Then certainly the true shall come,
And sow the seeds of peace.

SCARCE TRUTHS

SCARCE TRUTHS

This feral sphere has seldom turn'd
Without essence of pureness burn'd

Indeed pureness has been set alight.
Rare moments pass in this untamed world,
Without ideals of righteousness aflame.
Behold as the last flaring truth becomes dust,
Yet the dark fire long continues to feast.

The lustful zealots seek ill harm
A bid to seize her vestal charm

Overcome be the chaste queen,
No heed paid to Her exhausted pleas,
Lecherous savages ravage her virtuous crown,
Within order that betrays moral restraint,
Justice a mere forgotten trait.

As often does autumn foliage fall
So do Men piled large with small

How numerous the autumn leaves fall,
Far greater do Men perish,
Be they timid or bold,
Willing or unwise,
A fate alike in agony awaits.

Vast efforts conspire to conquer wisdom
Yet untouch'd be his knowing kingdom

Certainly these be irrefutable words.
He is the most high, the most just,
All be known by his wisdom infinite.
Mankind ever plans with the gifted mind,
Yet the greatest planner is he.

Story behind the poem

The idea behind the poem **Irony of Life** (on p. 94) explores the contradictory nature of emotions, where happiness can quickly turn to sadness. For me, when I'm feeling joyful, thinking about those who are less fortunate brings a sense of sadness alongside my joy.

US

I hope we strive for each,
To attain solace in life.
I pray that we succeed,
To be one in paradise.

YOU BLESSED MY EYES

YOU BLESSED MY EYES

Before I came, I brought too much pain.
You suffered me, but never once complained.
I must have worn you, all I did was weep.
You were so calm, and sung unto my sleep.
My beloved, precious tears you shed for me,
Wasted, so ungrateful, if only I could see.
When all the world shut close the doors,
There was no shoulder greater than yours.
My dreams are lost without you, O dearest,
For in the world, you were my nearest.
My eyes are longing to see you,
My ears are listening to hear you.
You were such beauty, wrapped in modesty.
You were such laughter, wrapped in piety.
When life was hell, you made it heaven,
And that's where we'll meet, of that I'm certain

PROFITS OF WAR

PROFITS OF WAR

I witness bombs being dropped,
Whole nations erased,
Innocents caught unawares,
No time to think.
No farewell to loved one's,
No kiss for their kids,
No choice, no reason,
Not allowed to blink.
Life seized from them,
Like it was never theirs.
A price paid for others
Obsession with gain.
With power, with money,
No care for their living,
No care for their suffering,
No care for their pain.

Deceiving mere mortals
With relentless propaganda.
Masking true intentions
Behind closed doors.
Gullibility believes them to be
Prophets of peace.
But all the devil wants
Is the profits of war.

UNSEEN BELIEF

UNSEEN BELIEF

See within the eyes of belief.
Become a guest in the mind of faith.
Allow one day from your many of madness,
To behold wondrous tranquility.
Let your heart rise in certainty,
Like the raging Sun abides,
And your gaze be lowered in awe,
As the trees in their might bow.
Witness the peaks unmoved,
And the unconquered stars,
Ever chaste they remain.
Hear as the wind honours,
And all the creatures sing,
Of one whom Man forgct.

DEATH UPON MY OWN

DEATH UPON MY OWN

Yes! Speak it as I write,
I wish death upon my own.
To all it seems a callous sin,
That I wish death upon my own.
The feeble young, the frailest old,
Alike I do wish death upon.
The gentle hand, the guiding soul,
To each I do wish death upon.
Know me not as one alone,
But I wish death upon my own.

No! I oppose not life,
Nor revel within sacrifice.
Yet bear the pain of pain,
Of all who seek in peace to live,
Not to endure a day enslaved,
To find true solace and escape,
Then I shall plead and I shall pray,
And wish for death upon my own.

A PRAYER

A PRAYER

O ALLAH heal the sick and frail,
Without your aid we surely fail.
To you our Lord indeed we pray,
Please lead the true to victors way.

PATHS OF LIFE

PATHS OF LIFE

Life is a myriad of errors.
A labyrinth with many paths.
It may not be forever pleasing,
Yet one must persevere,
For patience invariably finds,
The path where beauty lies.

WE ARE ONE

WE ARE ONE

Are we really so blind?
Are we truly so deaf?
What have we become.
When did empathy depart,
And love convert to hate
Yes, we shall condemn,
But we shall also delve within,
Our own ignorance and fears,
Our cruel and absent trust.
To disregard the other,
And ridicule their plights.
We tread upon the weak,
And sow the seeds of rage.

But now we shall unite,
And divide shall not remain.
We shall raise aloud our voice,
And not allow disgrace
We shall stand as one with all,
And cast afar each pain,
For we are one united race.

THE LAVISH PATH

Should I walk the lavish path,
Upon ways of gilded leaves,
Within vanity and laughter,
As the world beside me grieves?

WOEFUL JUDGMENT

WOEFUL JUDGMENT

What woeful judgment shall it be,
Upon who preaches honesty,
Yet speaks not truth but lies.
Alike shall be the ceaseless flame,
Upon who cause a Fathers pain,
And Mothers weeping eyes.

MY CHILD

MY CHILD

The first glimpse of you my child,
Such bliss overwhelmed my soul.
Your weeping was a soothing song,
That vanquished every pain of mine.
Enlivened was my weary heart,
By the purity in your joyful smile.
The warmth of your gentle touch,
Thawed my every bitterness.
Indeed my being was enriched,
By the solace of your coming.

INNER CROWN

INNER CROWN

She who reveres her inner crown,

Shall certainly be proclaimed Queen.

Who fortifies her abode,

And venerates her King,

With piety and truth.

Then indeed success shall arrive,

Within her every touch.

Each adverse eye shall behold,

A Queen atop her throne.

I AM PALESTINE

I AM PALESTINE

I weep as the world smiles,
Tears that never cease.
Proclaim me as humanity's child,
Yet never grant me peace.
I shall never bow nor give,
For I have seen the signs,
Of a day my soul shall live,
In restful Palestine.

FIRE

FIRE

Engulfed. Enraged.

Scorched and consumed.

Dark souls aflame.

Yet worthy hearts too shall blaze,

And set alight the way.

YOU AND ME

YOU AND ME

You and me were meant to be,
To hold each other lovingly,
To laugh, to love, to live as one,
And stay beyond the setting sun.
Search within my heart to see,
Two faithful lovers ever young.

SPIRITUAL SENSE

Though I am blind,

My eyes are as wide and open as the sky.

I can see through them.

And though I am deaf,

I hear as the Mother hears her child.

For my heart is pure,

And my faith is firm,

Thus, I am awake.

SIMPLE JOY

SIMPLE JOY

Gaze within my soul to see,

The many untold sides of me.

I am but a humble slave,

Who seeks not riches, neither fame,

Yet merely peace through goodness gained,

To live forever glad and free.

SUCCESS

SUCCESS

Being rich is not defined

By how much gold one possesses.

Rather,

True richness is defined by happiness.

If you have a wealth of joy

And contentment in your life.

Then you have found,

The true definition of success.

IRONY OF LIFE

When I am sad I get happy,
For I know this sadness
Will come to pass.
When I am happy I get sad,
For I know this happiness
Will seldom last.

CONTENTED SOUL

Embrace my restless being,
Hear my hearts tempted rhythm,
Feel the desire within my touch,
As your soul marries mine.

JOURNEY OF LIFE

Vast Is the journey of life.

Within it are many paths.

Many highs,

Many lows.

In every path you must seek

To make the world,

Brighter than you came.

MOON-CHILD

MOON-CHILD

She who glides among the winds,
And seeks the essence of the bloom,
Who merges with the oceans waves,
She, a child of the moon.

SLEEP AWAY THE HURT

I think your eyes must be tired.

Watching this crazy world

Create chaos,

And destroy order.

Watching Man smile,

Unremorseful,

While he inherits what was yours.

You have seen much already my friend.

Let your eye lashes embrace.

Let your mind be eased of all it's worries.

Let all your many burdens disappear.

A peaceful journey into the world of dreams.

Good night.

www.ingramcontent.com/pod-product-compliance
Ingram Content Group UK Ltd.
Pitfield, Milton Keynes, MK11 3LW, UK
UKHW051018070125
453272UK00009B/87